C.C.

The GROSS AND GOOFY Body

Here We Grow

The Secrets of Hair and Nails

By Melissa Stewart
Illustrated by Janet Hamlin

Marshall Cavendish
Benchmark
New York

THIS BOOK WAS MADE POSSIBLE,
IN PART, BY A GRANT FROM THE
SOCIETY OF CHILDREN'S BOOK WRITERS AND ILLUSTRATORS.

Published by Marshall Cavendish Benchmark
An imprint of Marshall Cavendish Corporation

This publication represents the opinions and views of the author based on Melissa Stewart's personal experience, knowledge, and research. The information in this book serves as a general guide only. The author and publisher have used their best efforts in preparing this book and disclaim liability rising directly and indirectly from the use and application of this book.

Other Marshall Cavendish Offices:
Marshall Cavendish International (Asia) Private Limited, 1 New Industrial Road, Singapore 536196 • Marshall Cavendish International (Thailand) Co Ltd. 253 Asoke, 12th Flr, Sukhumvit 21 Road, Klongtoey Nua, Wattana, Bangkok 10110, Thailand • Marshall Cavendish (Malaysia) Sdn Bhd, Times Subang, Lot 46, Subang Hi-Tech Industrial Park, Batu Tiga, 40000 Shah Alam, Selangor Darul Ehsan, Malaysia

Marshall Cavendish is a trademark of Times Publishing Limited

All websites were available and accurate when this book was sent to press.

Library of Congress Cataloging-in-Publication Data
Stewart, Melissa.
Here we grow : the secrets of hair and nails / by Melissa Stewart.
p. cm. — (The gross and goofy body)
Includes index.
Summary: "Provides comprehensive information on the role hair and nails play in the body science of humans and animals" — Provided by the publisher.
ISBN 978-0-7614-4172-4
1. Hair — Juvenile literature. 2. Nails (Anatomy) — Juvenile literature.
I. Title.
QM488.S74 2010
612.7'99 — dc22
2008033563

Editor: Joy Bean
Publisher: Michelle Bisson
Art Director: Anahid Hamparian
Series Designer: Daniel Roode

Photo research by Tracey Engel
Cover photo: Getty Images/Digital Vision/David Sacks

Printed in Malaysia (T)
135642

CONTENTS

THE PERFECT PROTECTORS

What protects your body from the outside world? Your skin, of course. But it doesn't do the job all on its own.

The thick, heavy hair growing out of your scalp keeps your head warm and dry. And it helps shield your head from thuds, thumps, bangs, and bumps.

Your fingers and toes need extra protection, too. Luckily, hard, tough nails save the day. They guard the tender tips of your fingers and toes from scrapes and scratches.

Think that's all your hair and nails do for you? Think again! Even though they're dead, they still have many important jobs to do. You'll be amazed at all the ways hair and nails make life better for you—and for other animals, too.

A polar bear's white fur blends in perfectly with its snowy surroundings. It helps the hungry hunter catch its **prey** by surprise.

What does a lioness think when she sees a lion with a long, thick mane? "Hubba hubba, you'd make a great mate."

Monkeys use their fingernails to pick dead skin, insects, and dirt out of their friends' fur. It's the perfect way to stay clean and build trust.

HAIR, HAIR EVERYWHERE

Who has a hairier body—you or a gorilla?

Don't answer too fast. It's a trick question.

Gorillas are great apes—our closest relatives in the animal world. And it turns out that we have the same amount of hair—about 5 million strands—sticking out of our skin.

Why do gorillas look so much hairier? Because it's easy to spot the thick, dark locks that make up a gorilla's fur. But you hardly even notice the short, thin **vellus hairs** covering your body.

Look for vellus hairs like these growing all over your body.

If you're wondering why human body hair is so slender and slight, you aren't alone. Nobody knows for sure. But scientists have some ideas.

• Apes spend several hours a day picking ticks, lice, and other pesky pests out of their fur. Ugh! That's disgusting! Thin, short hair would have saved prehistoric people time, energy, and a whole lot of aggravation.

• Early humans lived on Africa's sizzling savannas. Short, thin hair would have helped them stay cool.

• Our ancient **ancestors** probably spent a lot of time wading through water in search of food. Thick, heavy hair would have really weighed them down.

WHO HAS HAIR?

Fish don't have hair. They have scales. So do reptiles. And everybody knows that birds have feathers.

If you're looking for hair, you'll need to find a **mammal**. Bears and beavers, platypuses and porcupines, cats, and kangaroos all have thick, lush fur. Even elephants and whales have a little bit of hair.

What determines how much hair a mammal has? The size of its body and where it lives.

Large animals heat up faster than small ones. That's why elephants, hippos, and rhinos have much less hair than do mongooses and hyenas.

Whales and walruses often swim in chilly seas, so wet, matted fur would really slow them down. Instead, a thick layer of blubber keeps them warm.

Naked mole rats are smaller than chipmunks, so why don't they have thick, furry coats? Because they live underground, and their tunnels stay toasty warm all year long.

Furry Facts

Most mammals have furry coats made of three kinds of hair. The thick top coat is made mostly of **awn hairs**. Scattered here and there are longer, coarser **guard hairs**. They repel water, so the animal stays dry. A mammal's undercoat contains thin, fluffy **down hairs**. These trap warm air close to the animal's skin.

LONG LASHES, BUSHY BROWS

Has your mom ever given you the hairy eyeball? It's when she squints her eyes and lowers her lids, so her eyelashes pop out at you. That look means she knows you're up to something, but she isn't sure what.

When your sister lowers both eyebrows, look out! It means she's angry. And when your dad raises one eyebrow, be prepared. He thinks you're telling a lie.

Long lashes and bushy brows do more than express feelings. They also protect your delicate eyes.

While you are awake, your eyelids usually blink thirty to sixty times a minute. That adds up to more than thirty thousand times a day, and ten million times a year. Each time, your eyelashes flick away tiny bits of dust and dirt. Not bad for a bunch of tiny hairs!

On rainy days your eyebrows trap the raindrops trickling down your forehead. On hot days they soak up salty sweat before it stings your eyes. Thank goodness for those thick, hairy tufts!

Bugged by Itchy Eyes

Ever had itchy eyes? That frustrating feeling might have been caused by *Demodex*, tiny mites that live on people's eyelashes. Ew! Gross!

How can you get rid of those itty-bitty bugs? Wash your face every day.

WHAT'S A WHISKER?

You have probably noticed the long, stiff hairs on either side of a cat's nose. Take a closer look, and you'll see even more of those wispy **whiskers** above a cat's eyes and below its mouth.

Cats aren't the only animals with whiskers. Dogs have them, too. So do rats and bats and most other mammals. Whiskers help mammals sense their surroundings. But different animals use their whiskers in different ways.

Some bats have whiskers on their butts. Yup, their butts! The bristly hairs help the nighttime fliers land in tight spaces.

If something brushes against a dog's whiskers, it closes its eyes, shakes its head, and pulls away.

A walrus's whiskers comb the muddy seafloor in search of clams, snails, and other tasty treats.

Seals use their whiskers to sense the movement of fish.

When a cat pounces on prey, its whiskers move forward to form a net in front of its mouth. The web of whiskers helps the hunter keep track of its meal.

The whiskers on a squirrel's ankles help it avoid bumping into branches as it jumps from tree to tree.

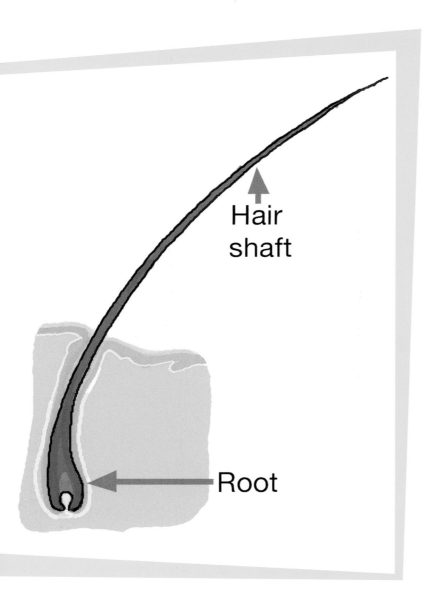

Hair shaft

Root

Grab a hair and pluck it out of your head. What you'll see is a long, smooth thread with a grayish white knob at the end. That little lump is the **root**, the part of your hair that's normally inside your skin. The rest of the strand is called the **hair shaft**.

Pinch the root of your hair, and run your fingers along the shaft. What you're feeling is the **cuticle**, your hair's outermost layer. It's made of flat, colorless cells that overlap like the shingles on a roof.

Your hair's hard, tough cuticle protects a thick inner layer called the **cortex**. Your cortex contains most of the **pigments** that give your hair its color.

If the hairs on your head are black, brown, or red, each strand has a soft, spongy center called the **medulla**. It contains some pigments and lots of air pockets. Blond hairs don't have medullas. Neither do body hairs.

Tattered Tresses

Sun, salt, and too much brushing mean big trouble for your lovely locks. They wear away the protective cuticle, leaving behind a frayed frizzle. How do you get rid of those split ends? There's just one way. Get out the scissors and *snip, snip*!

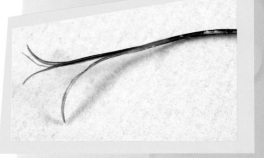

UNDER YOUR SKIN

Before you yank a poor little hair out of your head, its root is nestled—safe and snug—inside a **hair follicle**.

The bulging bulb at the bottom of a hair follicle is packed with dozens of tiny **blood vessels**. They supply nearby hair cells with the **oxygen** and **nutrients** they need to live and grow.

Living hair cells divide to create new cells every twenty-three to seventy-two hours. That's faster than any other cells in your body.

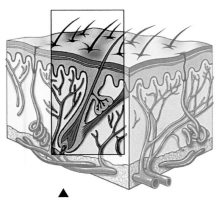

Follicle with hair ▶

▲
**Cross section
of skin**

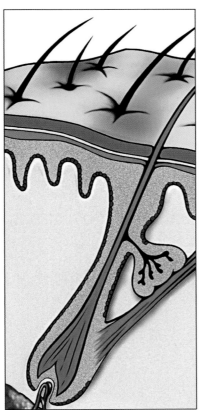

As new hair cells form, they push the older cells up and out of your follicle. The farther these cells move, the less oxygen and nutrients they receive.

Eventually, the older cells begin to die. But before they go kaput, they crank out as much **keratin** as they can. Tough and strong, keratin helps dead hair cells last longer before flaking off.

Oozing Oil

Most dead cells are dry and brittle. So why is your hair so soft and flexible? Because a thin layer of oily **sebum** coats your hair. Sebum is constantly trickling out of small sacs attached to your hair follicles. The oozing oil keeps your hair strong, shiny, and waterproof.

STRAIGHT OR CURLY?

You've probably heard of **DNA**. It's the genetic material inside your cells.

DNA contains a set of instructions that you **inherited**, or received, from your parents. It determines all kinds of body traits, including the size of your ears, the shape of your nose, and how tall you'll grow.

When it comes to hair, DNA makes all the decisions—from texture and strength to color and length.

- If your ancestors lived in Africa, your DNA probably contains instructions for making long, thin hair follicles. They produce hair that is kinky and breaks easily.

- If your ancestors lived in Asia or the Americas, you probably have round hair follicles that produce strong, straight strands.

- If your ancestors lived in Europe, your hair follicles are probably oval. That's why your hair is wavy or curly and fairly strong.

How Slowly Does It Grow?

While a hair is growing, cells move up and out of your follicle fast enough for the stringy strand to lengthen about 6 inches (15 centimeters) per year. Strong, straight hair grows the fastest, and fragile, kinky hair grows the slowest.

THE MAGIC OF MELANIN

What color is your hair? That question probably seems like a no-brainer, but don't answer too quickly. Take a good, long look in the mirror first.

People might say your hair is brown, but is every single hair really that color? Most likely, some strands are blond or red or black.

A pigment called **melanin** gives your hair its color. It's located in the cortex—and sometimes the medulla—of every single hair on your head.

It sounds pretty simple, but it's not. There are two kinds of melanin, and one is darker than the other.

If you're a blonde, most of your hairs contain the lighter pigment. And if you're a brunette, most of your hairs contain the darker pigment. Nearly everyone has a mix of the two types.

What determines the pattern of darker and lighter hairs sprinkled across your head? Your DNA, of course.

Going Gray

As people get older, their hair produces less melanin. Gray hairs contain just a little bit of melanin. White hairs contain no melanin at all.

Most people begin going gray when they're around thirty, but some start much earlier or later. Like just about everything else, it depends on DNA.

CALLING IT QUITS

Right now, you have about 100,000 hairs sticking out of your scalp. About 85,000 of them are growing. The rest are either taking a break or getting ready to fall out.

Thanks to the instructions in DNA, some people's head hairs stop growing after just two years. Their hair never even reaches their shoulders. But in other people, hairs keep on growing for seven years or more.

All of these women have hair that is more than 6 feet (2 meters) long.

How long do you think your hair would grow if you never cut it? A Chinese girl named Xie Qiuping asked herself that question in 1973, when she was thirteen years old. Today, her hair is more than 18 feet (5 meters) long. That's more than three times longer than she is tall!

When a hair stops growing, it rests for ten days to three months. Then it breaks and falls out, and a new hair starts growing.

Lost Locks

You lose about a hundred hairs every day. But you probably don't even notice. That's because new hairs start to grow right away.

Some people aren't so lucky. Many older men—and some older women—stop growing new hairs on some parts of their head. What makes some people go bald while others don't? You guessed it—DNA.

CHANGING COATS

You lose your hair one strand at a time. But most mammals molt, or shed their fur, all at once.

A seal spends most of its life in the ocean. But for about a month each year, it moves onto land and **molts**. It doesn't eat. It doesn't drink. It just lies around, waiting for its old coat to fall off and a silky new one to grow in.

During their autumn molt, weasels and snowshoe hares turn off their melanin-making cells. That gives them a white winter coat that blends in with snow. During the spring molt, their melanin-making cells crank up production. That's why their summer coats are brown—perfect for hiding in grass or under shrubs.

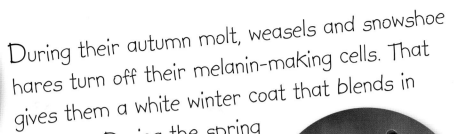

Dogs and cats shed their coats twice a year. As the days grow longer and warmer in spring, their thick winter fur falls out in clumps. The summer coat that grows in is thinner. In autumn, as the days grow shorter and cooler, dogs and cats shed their summer coat. Heavier fur grows in to keep them toasty warm all winter long.

A fawn's first coat is speckled with spots that help the baby animal blend in with its surroundings. By late summer, a young deer can run as fast as its parents. So during the autumn molt, it loses its spots.

BLENDING IN, STICKING OUT

Even when hair doesn't change with the seasons, it can still help animals hide from their predators— and their prey. It can also help animals attract mates or send messages.

What color is a pocket mouse's fur? That depends on where it lives. If it spends most of its time on dark lava rock, its coat is black. But if it lives in a sandy place, its fur is light yellow. A pocket mouse's hair always matches its surroundings.

A tiger's black stripes and orange fur make it hard to spot. It can sneak through the grass and catch its prey by surprise.

In the thick, dark forests where mandrills live, it's hard for monkeys to see one another. So a male mandrill depends on its pale beard and colorful face to catch a female's attention.

When zebras run in a group, their stripes blend together. That makes it hard for **predators** to tell where one zebra ends and another begins.

As a deer flees from danger, its bouncing white tail tells other animals they should run, too.

A skunk's white stripe makes it easy to spot. It warns other animals to stay away.

CAN'T BEAR THAT HAIR

The hair on your head sends signals. If it looks great, it says, "Hey, I'm happy and healthy. You'll like hanging out with me." But if it's dull and dirty, people will think you just don't care. That's why Americans spend billions of dollars on their hair every year.

Facial and body hair is a different story. Most people don't want it, and they can't get rid of it fast enough. That's how it's been for thousands of years.

6000 B.C.E. to 2000 C.E.

Ancient Sumeria

People removed facial hair with tweezers.

4000 B.C.E. to 1397 C.E. Ancient India

Men removed the hair on their chests. Women removed the hair on their legs.

3100 B.C.E. to 31 B.C.E. Ancient Egypt

Men used bronze and copper razors. Women used hair-removal creams made of beeswax and starch.

1100 B.C.E. to 146 B.C.E. Ancient Greece

Men shaved their faces daily. Women singed hair off their legs with lamps.

146 B.C.E. to 476 C.E. Ancient Rome

Men shaved their faces daily. Women plucked their eyebrows and used hair-removal creams made from tree sap, donkey fat, bat blood, and other strange ingredients.

Hair to the Rescue !

American salons cut almost 200 tons (181,437 kg) of hair every day. They used to throw away the clippings, but now they send them to environmental groups, so they can be used to clean up oil spills. That's really using your head!

29

THAT NAILS IT

Fingernails. Think of all the ways you use them every day. They're perfect for scraping away crusty eye gunk and scratching an itchy head. You use them to scoop dead, flaking skin out of your ears and to pick up small objects, such as pennies. And sometimes—even though you know you shouldn't—you use your fingernails to pick a scab or flick boogers out of your nose.

Believe it or not, your fingernails—and your toenails, too—have a lot in common with your hair. They all grow out of your skin, and they're all made of dead cells full of keratin.

And like the hair on your head, your nifty nails protect delicate body parts. They also add strength and stiffness to the tender tips of your fingers and toes.

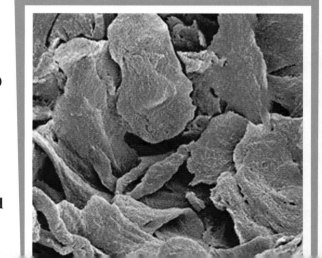

A close-up look at the dead cells in a fingernail.

Don't Crunch and Munch

Ever bitten your nails when you felt bored or nervous? It's not a healthy habit.

If your nails are too short, they can't do their job. All that chewing and chomping can break open your skin. Then all kinds of nasty **germs** can sneak into your body and make you sick.

NAILS UP CLOSE

Even though you use your nails dozens of times a day, you've probably never taken a close look at them. Now's your chance.

The first thing you'll notice is your **nail plate**—the hard, tough sheet covering each fingertip. Its lower surface has grooves that anchor it to a thick layer of skin called the **nail bed**.

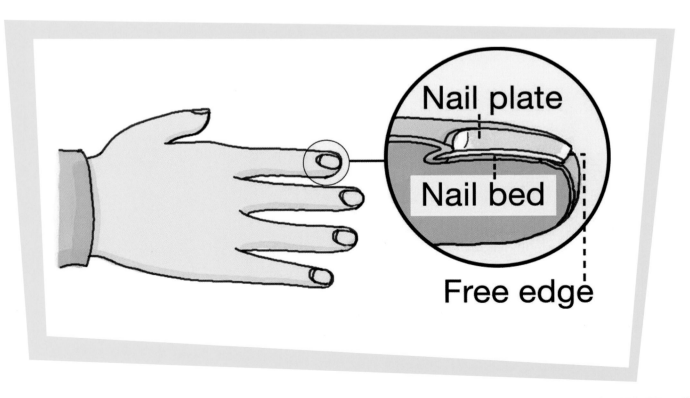

Nail plate

Nail bed

Free edge

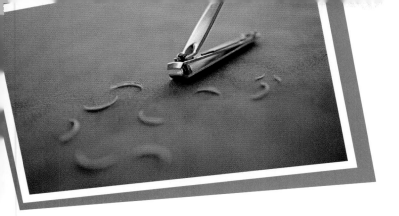

The part of the nail plate that extends beyond the nail bed is called the **free edge**. It's what you carefully clip off every once in a while.

Now look for a white half circle near the base of your nail. It's easiest to see on your thumbnail and big toe. This **lunula** is the top edge of the nail root. The rest of the root is hidden by the skin at the bottom of your nail.

free edge

lunula

On the Edge

Your skin doesn't just end along the sides of your nails. It folds under and merges into your nail bed. That skin and the cuticle at the bottom of your nail act like shock absorbers. They also help to keep water and bacteria out of your body.

RECORD-SETTING NAILS

Lee Redmond

Like your hair follicles, your nail roots contain living cells. As they divide, the new cells push older cells out of the root and across your nail bed. That's what makes your nails grow.

It takes about six months for a fingernail to grow from its root to the free edge. So imagine how long it's been since Lee Redmond, a woman from Salt Lake City, Utah, cut her record-setting nails. At 28 to 31 inches (71 to 79 cm) apiece, her tremendous talons drag on the ground.

Louise Hollis of Compton, California, has set a world's record of her own. She hasn't cut her toenails since 1981. Today they're between 6 and 9 inches (15 and 23 cm) long. Now that's incredible!

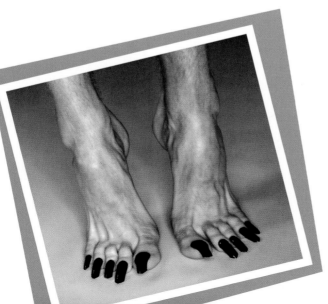

Look how long these toenails are! Do you think they'll beat Louise Hollis's world record?

Cold Hands, Warm Heart

Do you ever remember a time when your body didn't feel cold but your hands did? At times such as that, you should look at your fingernails. You'll see that they're turning blue. What's going on?

When your body is fighting to stay warm, it pumps extra blood to your most important **organs**. Very little blood flows to your fingers and toes. As the oxygen in your blood is used up and **carbon dioxide** forms, your blood darkens and your nail beds start to look blue.

FAST AND FURIOUS

Think you cut your fingernails more often than your toenails? Nope, it's not your imagination. Fingernails really do grow faster—usually three times faster.

Fingernails grow about 1 inch (2.5 cm) every eight months, but some grow faster than others. The nail on your middle finger grows the fastest. The nails on your thumb and little finger grow the slowest.

Fingernails grow more quickly during the day and in the summer. And they grow faster on whichever hand you use most—probably because lots of muscle flexing really heats things up.

What a Pain !

Your big toe hurts, and it sure is swollen. You lift your foot and take a closer look.

Instead of growing straight, your nail plate has curved down. The sharp edge is cutting into your nail bed. No wonder you're in pain!

Lots of things can cause an ingrown toenail—stubbing your toe, cutting the nail too short, wearing tight shoes.

What should you do? Tell an adult right away. Then soak your toe three or four times a day and wear comfortable shoes. Before you know it, your toenail should be back on track.

NOT QUITE NAILS

Like you, monkeys and apes have nails at the tips of their fingers and toes. But most four-legged animals have **claws** instead. Animals use their claws in many different ways. A cat's claws are perfect for catching and holding prey. Squirrels and raccoons use their claws to scurry up trees. And when a prairie dog wants to dig a hole, its claws do the job.

Claws have a lot in common with nails, but they're made of two layers of cells—not just one. The hard outer layer is just like your nail plate. The soft, flaky bottom layer grows more slowly. That's why claws are curved but nails are straight.

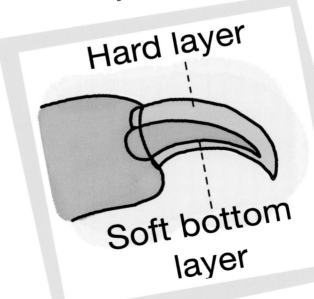

Hard layer

Soft bottom layer

Ever looked at a horse's feet? They don't have claws, and they don't have nails. Like hippos, camels, cattle, and deer, horses have **hooves**—layers of thick, hard keratin that surround the tips of an animal's toes. Hard, tough hooves support an animal's body weight and allow it to run fast.

Withdraw That Claw!

What does your cat do when it's feeling friendly? Your purring pet pulls its claws inside its paws. That way it won't scratch you by mistake.

HAIR AND NAILS TELL TALES

When you're healthy, your nails usually are, too. And if your body is in trouble, your nails may let you know.

If your nails curl around your fingers, there may be something wrong with your heart or lungs. If your nails break easily, you may not be eating right or you may have an infection. And if your nails seem to sink into your nail beds, you may not have enough oxygen in your blood.

This is what a hair shaft looks like under a powerful microscope.

Hair tells tales, too, but you need to look closely to see them. When scientists view hair strands under a microscope, they can tell whether a person smokes cigarettes, drinks alcohol, or takes illegal drugs. They can also tell a person's ethnic background.

From diagnosing diseases and picking up objects to keeping us safe and snug, it's hard to believe all the ways hair and nails help us every day. And we aren't alone. Many other animals depend on them, too.

Hair and Nails Solve Crimes

Lost hairs and nail clippings might seem useless to you, but they aren't to police. When officers find them at a crime scene, they get very excited. They can use the DNA in hairs and nails to identify suspects.

POLICE DO NOT CROSS

GLOSSARY

ancestor—A person who lived before you and from whom you are descended.

awn hair—A medium-length hair that helps to insulate an animal and protect its soft down hair.

blood vessel—One of the tubes that carries blood throughout the body.

carbon dioxide—An invisible gas that animals make as they get energy from food.

claw—The hard, sharp structure on the tip of most animal toes. It consists of two layers of cells.

cortex—The middle or innermost layer of hair. It contains pigment cells.

cuticle—In hair, the outermost protective layer. In nails, a protective layer of cells where the nail meets the skin.

DNA (deoxyribonucleic acid)—A molecule with instructions that direct all the activities in a cell. It is passed from parent to child during reproduction.

down hair—A soft hair that grows close to the skin. It traps air to help keep an animal warm.

free edge—The part of a nail that extends beyond the nail bed.

germ—A tiny organism or particle that can make people sick.

guard hair—A long, coarse hair that is waterproof.

hair follicle—The tube from which a hair strand grows.

hair shaft—The portion of the hair strand that is outside the skin.

hoof—A tough, nail-like structure that surrounds the tip of some animals' toes and acts like a foot.

inherit—To receive from an ancestor.

keratin—The main ingredient in dead hair and nail cells.

lunula—The white, curved area at the bottom of a nail.

mammal—An animal with a backbone and hair. Mammalian mothers feed their babies milk that they make inside their bodies. Humans are mammals.

medulla—The central part of some animal hairs.

melanin—The pigment that gives skin, hair, and eyes their color.

molt—To lose or shed hair or other body coverings.

nail bed—The thick skin below the nail plate.

nail plate—A hard, flat sheet that covers and protects the tip of a finger or toe.

nutrient—A substance that keeps the body healthy. It comes from food.

organ—A body part made up of several kinds of tissue that work together. The heart, lungs, and brain are organs.

oxygen—An invisible gas that animals need to live.

pigment—A naturally colored material.

predator—An animal that hunts and kills other animals for food.

prey—An animal that is hunted by a predator.

root—In a hair, the part that's below the skin. Hair grows out of a follicle inside each hair root. In a nail, the area that contains living cells. As those cells divide, the nail grows.

sebum—The oil that keeps skin and hair soft, moist, and a little bit waterproof.

vellus hair—One of the short, thin hairs covering the body.

whisker—A long, stiff hair that some animals use to sense their surroundings.

A NOTE ON SOURCES

Dear Readers,

Who knew hair and nails could be so interesting? I certainly didn't before I started doing research for this book. Very few books have been written about hair or nails, so tracking down all the information was no easy task. Still, I had a lot of fun doing it.

Most of the information about the structure, function, and growth of human hair and nails came from medical textbooks and scientific papers. That's how I learned about ingrown toenails, the dangers of biting your nails, and how nails can be used to diagnose diseases. Some of the most fun facts came from the *Guinness Book of World Records*. I included them because kids asked me to. They also wanted to know more about fur, claws, and hooves, and I was happy to oblige by scouring books that focus on animal behavior.

Other information came from popular science magazines, the Internet, or interviews with scientists. And a reference librarian at the Massachusetts Institute of Technology helped me track down information about the history of hair removal. Thank goodness for librarians!

—Melissa Stewart

FIND OUT MORE

BOOKS

Amazing Animals of the World. New York: Scholastic Library, 2006.

Green, Jen. *Skin, Hair and Hygiene.* Corona, CA: Stargazer Books, 2005.

Miles, Elizabeth. *Fur and Feathers.* Chicago: Heinemann, 2002.

WEBSITES

Guinness World Records
This site provides up-to-date information on some of the strangest world records you can imagine.
http://www.guinnessworldrecords.com/default.aspx

Kids Health
This site answers just about any question you might have about your body and keeping it healthy.
http://kidshealth.org/kid/

Oil Spill Hair Mats
Learn about one of the amazing ways environmental scientists are using human hair cuttings.
http://www.matteroftrust.org/programs/natural.html

That Explains It!
This site contains all kinds of interesting information about the human body, animals, food, inventions and machines, and more.
http://www.coolquiz.com/trivia/explain/

INDEX

Page numbers in **bold** are illustrations.

ABOUT THE AUTHOR

Melissa Stewart has written everything from board books for preschoolers to magazine articles for adults. She is the award-winning author of more than one hundred books for young readers. She serves on the board of advisors of the Society of Children's Book Writers and Illustrators and is a judge for the American Institute of Physics Children's Science Writing Award. Stewart earned a B.S. in biology from Union College and an M.A. in science journalism from New York University. She lives in Acton, Massachusetts, with her husband, Gerard. To learn more about Stewart, please visit her website: www.melissa-stewart.com.

ABOUT THE ILLUSTRATOR

Janet Hamlin has illustrated many children's books, games, newspapers, and even Harry Potter stuff. She is also a court artist. The Gross and Goofy Body is one of her all-time favorite series, and she now considers herself the factoid queen of bodily functions. She lives and draws in New York and loves it.